Your Steps are ordered of Me Saith the Lord

A Journey with the Holy Spirit

Your Steps are ordered of Me Saith the Lord

A Journey with the Holy Spirit

Joshua & Maureen Pfister

Copyright © 2001 by
Joshua and Maureen Pfister

All rights reserved. No part of this book shall be reproduced or transmitted in any form or by any means, electronic, mechanical, magnetic, photographic including photocopying, recording or by any information storage and retrieval system, without prior written permission of the publisher. No patent liability is assumed with respect to the use of the information contained herein. Although every precaution has been taken in the preparation of this book, the publisher and author assume no responsibility for errors or omissions. Neither is any liability assumed for damages resulting from the use of the information contained herein.

ISBN 0-7414-0644-6

Published by:

INFINITY
PUBLISHING.COM

Infinity Publishing.com
519 West Lancaster Avenue
Haverford, PA 19041-1413
Info@buybooksontheweb.com
www.buybooksontheweb.com
Toll-free (877) BUY BOOK
Local Phone (610) 520-2500
Fax (610) 519-0261

Printed in the United States of America

Printed on Recycled Paper

Published May, 2001

We would like to dedicate this book to our families. You have been so loving and supporting. We love you, Denny (Dad) & Shari (Mom), Matt, Mark & Roxanne, Michelle, Doyle III & Dana, and Rachel.

Our deepest appreciation to...

The LORD God Almighty; without You we could do nothing and this book would have never been written. We love You!

Our dear friends, Gary and Jeanine Meyer, for the countless hours they spent with us helping and encouraging us through the process of this book. You two are great!

Michael Carmody for going out to the front lines with us. We love you; keep up the good work!

Donna Good for typing the testimonies; it gave us a great start.

Bill Preachuk for an awesome job editing.

All our partners and friends for all your prayers and encouragement. You are the best and we love and appreciate you all!

Contents

About the Authors i
Introduction iii
1. The Holy Spirit Seen As 1
    Love & Compassion 3
    The Comforter 7
    Faithful 9
    Hope 14
    Power 16
    The Loving Rebuker 22
    Truth 27
2. Train'n Ground 29
3. God's Timing 35
4. His Leading 47
5. Conclusion 55

About the Authors

Have you ever wondered, "Where is the power of God these days? Are the things the Holy Spirit did through man a thing of the past? Does God decide to move only at rare times through a few special people?"

Joshua and Maureen Pfister are the most usual people you could meet, and yet the most unusual couple you would ever meet. Let me explain. Josh and Maureen would not visually stand out in a crowd. You could easily walk past them in a restaurant, bus or airplane. Except, this couple may not walk past you in a restaurant, bus, or airplane if you have been asking God for answers to problems in your life. They may be sent in the middle of the night to your door... even if your door happens to be in Tanzania Africa, Mexico City or in a bar in South Minneapolis, Minnesota on a snow blown and cold night, with a message from the Holy Spirit that will change your life.

This couple moves when the Holy Spirit tells them, "turn right" or "turn left;" when He directs, they even give Him control of their car. Yes Virginia, the Lord of heaven and earth and all of creation, will today, move that creation for those who cry out for Him. He moves through everyone who will allow him to do so.

The compilation of events is in this book because these two individuals separately gave their lives—not just that nice saying you may hear in church on Sunday, but **their lives**; I mean 24/7 (24 hours a day 7 days a week) to **The LORD** to do with as He desires.

If you meet this couple, it will be God ordained, and you will sense that you have known them all your life. This will be the Holy Spirit in them you are attracted to that's pulling you into a similar relationship with Him. I wish that Joshua and Maureen were not unusual; God does not want them to be. He wants to move through everyone who will give themselves to Him 24/7; He wants this to be His usual affect on believers.

The written recounting of events listed here are only those that were recorded just prior to and during the assembly of this book. As Josh and Maureen would call us continually with the excitement of how the Holy Spirit had worked through them, the Spirit of God spoke and said to our hearts that it was time to publish and encourage others!

GOD IS WORKING THROUGH BELEIVERS TODAY AND WANTS TO WORK THROUGH YOU AS WELL—TODAY!

Gary & Jeanine Meyer

Introduction

One day a man was in prayer, praying as he had done so often before, for "lost souls to come to a salvation knowledge of Jesus Christ," when he had a vision.

He was sitting at the feet of Jesus as he saw a line of faceless people, as far as the eye could see, walking up to a black hole which opened to Hell. They were unaware of its horror walking, talking and laughing, until they were about to fall. Then, seeing what was about to happen, they would scream for help.

I began to pray to Jesus to save them—"Lord," I said, "the prayers of a righteous man availeth much—save these people." The Lord, looking at me said, "Look at Me; now look at the people." I was surprised by His response to my prayer, as the line kept moving forward, and the screams of these people were loud and desperate. Jesus, I thought, You need to save them, as I looked at the always-moving souls marching to eternal damnation, pain and suffering.

This time, when I looked, the people were no longer faceless, but I recognized people I had seen, or had known, or met at one time during my life. Faces of people I had met at street corners, on buses, during sporting events and at church.

I turned, fell on my face and began to pray with great urgency, while hearing now familiar voices scream.

Suddenly, I couldn't pray any longer and I turned to catch them and tried to pull them out of the hole, even as they screamed that they were beginning to burn. I cried out to Jesus to help me, but before I could turn to look at Him, I saw my own family in line. I screamed in anguish!

I was desperately screaming and crying to Jesus to please help me as I tried to stop the line from moving. As I looked to where Jesus was sitting, I saw Him in tears and heard Him say, "NOW pray, Lord of the harvest—send laborers into the path of *my* family as I go into the paths of others you have sent me to."

Then Jesus said back to me—"My son, the effective FERVENT prayer of a righteous man availeth much!"

I believe that this book in the hands of any believer can spark a move of the Holy Spirit through evangelism in their life. If you need a fire started or rekindled, the testimonies in this book will do it!

We may never meet you in person, but we thought of you as we wrote this book. Our desire is to show you that the Holy Spirit can and will use anyone who is willing and obedient to do as He asks.

We've been called to be "watchmen," as the Prophet Ezekiel talks about (See Ezekiel 3:16-21 & 33:1-11). In time past, a watchman stood on the wall of a city and saw enemies coming and warned the population. We can see the destruction that awaits so many people. We must be faithful "watchmen" to speak to those who need warning. We need to obey those even seemingly small promptings of the Holy Spirit, as we remember, it's people's souls literally being saved from Hell.

So, let's be faithful to heed the promptings of the Holy Spirit, and receive His boldness that's spoken of in Psalm

138 where David proclaims, "You answered me, and made me bold with strength in my soul."

I believe that many Christians today have not grasped what they have in Christ. The Holy Spirit was sent to reveal Him to the world. He wants us to walk in the fullness of who He is! The only way the world is going to see Him is through us, so we need to reflect and imitate Him. We are a vessel carrying the goods! We are but a shell, full of the Spirit of God, waiting patiently to burst forth!

One

The Holy Spirit Seen As...

One day the Holy Spirit asked me, "who do you say I am and what proof is there that I live in you?" I took a hard look at myself, pondering on the questions He had asked me. I thought, "Am I reflecting the Lord? Am I being led by His Spirit, seeing those signs, wonders, and miracles that Jesus spoke about?" I said, "Lord, I want people to know that You are real. I want them to know that *You* have sent me to them." I began to cry out to God, "Reveal Yourself through me, make Yourself known," and He did.

The gift of knowledge, and faith to carry it out became stronger. He began to call us out to certain places and specific people while in prayer. As we waited on Him, He revealed His will to us. We went forth proclaiming the word He had spoken to us. We would arrive at our destination and say, "the Holy Spirit sent us to you. You need a miracle" or whatever else needed to be said at that time. People were speechless as they listened to what the Holy Spirit revealed to us about them.

The Spirit of God is waiting for us to say, "Yes Lord!" No matter how ridiculous it seems, or how far fetched it looks, He wants us to be obedient to do what we hear from Him. As you read these testimonies, I pray that you will be moved to compassion to say, "Yes Lord! Work through me that I may be sent to someone who needs to hear from you!"

The following testimonies will reveal the traits of the Holy Spirit as He has led us on this journey to reach out to find those who were lost and hurting.

Love & Compassion

A light of hope comes in the midnight hour.

It was a Thursday night and we were on our way to North Minneapolis to evangelize when the Lord said, "No, I want you to go to South Minneapolis." So we went to South Minneapolis and He said, "I want you to take your team and walk all the way down this road; I'm going to take you to a house." What's exciting is we never know exactly what to expect, but we know when God calls its going to be good because there is a purpose.

I could kind of see the house in my spirit so we walked and walked. We took a little turn to the left, and there on the corner was the house with a little light burning in the window. I knocked on the door and a lady came. I told her my name and said, "the Holy Ghost has sent me to you tonight and He's got a miracle for you." The woman's head was bowed really low and I sensed such depression over her. I said, "Do you know Jesus as your personal Lord and Savior?"

"Yes, I do."

"How do you know?"

"Well, I received Jesus into my heart and I know He's forgiven me of my sins."

"But I know that the Holy Ghost has sent me here to you tonight. Are you sick?"

"Well, I just got out of the hospital today."

"What's the problem?"

And with such shame she muttered, "I had an abortion." When she said that, I could feel the overwhelming love of God well up in me for her; I could feel the pain of her shame.

All day long the devil had been beating her up. He was saying things like, *"How could you kill something that you love? How could you call yourself a Christian and yet murder something God created and gave you? How could you? How could you? How could you?"* All day long she sank deeper and deeper into depression.

But God saw her. I said to her, "Have you asked God to forgive you?"

She said, "Yes, but I don't feel forgiven."

I said, "You've got to forgive yourself; Jesus has forgiven you. He sent us personally to you today to tell you that He loves you. He has forgiven you, and He sent us because you couldn't believe it. He knows your name, where you live, and what you did, but yet, He still forgave you when you asked Him. That's how much he loves you!"

At that moment the Holy Spirit took my arms and put them around her and held her. The Holy Spirit really ministered to her. Her whole countenance changed! Before leaving she said, "thank you; I know that God has forgiven me now. Him sending you here showed me how much He really loves me."

As I walked away from there that night the Holy Spirit said, "There's a lot of young girls out there tonight who have had abortions, whose daddies are pastors or they go to youth group and they are afraid to tell anybody. They're depressed and that's why they turn to drugs and alcohol; that's why they turn away from Me, because they're carrying that load." Then He said, "I want you to go and share My love to them."

FROM: *Jesus*

God showed us about this divine appointment about two weeks before it would happen.

He told us that on Christmas Day at 1 AM, we were going to meet a man downtown. We discovered through prayer that he was lonely and somewhat downtrodden and needed help. Then God said that morning before we went, "Get a box of chocolates as a present for this man, and tell him it's a Christmas present from Jesus."

We got a nice box of candies that had a Christmas wrap on it. We prayed going down there and were ready for what the Lord had planned. It was deserted and cold that night as we entered downtown. We pulled up and parked by a bus stop and saw a couple of people in the rear view mirror walking toward the car. Then they went into the bus shelter. The man had been drinking and was a little bit obnoxious. He began to say some off-the-wall things but we knew that this was the man that God brought us down to minister to.

The man said mockingly, "Do you got a Christmas present for me?"

"Yes we do," we said, "we have a Christmas present from Jesus for you." We told him the Holy Spirit sent us to him personally that Christmas night to give it to him. He seemed to be a little taken back and held the candy to his chest and then left us. The Lord showed us that he was going to wake up the next morning and see the box of candies. Then he would see how much Jesus loved him and had not forgotten him!

Where's your final destination?

I was getting ready to take a trip to Bulgaria a couple years ago when God spoke to my heart while in prayer. He said, "There's going to be someone on the plane I want you to meet. I want you to ask her, 'If the plane was to go down today, where would you spend eternity?'" I was so excited and could hardly wait.

I go all the way to Bulgaria and nothing happened. On the way back, we stopped off in Austria. It was a quick stop over; a few people got on and off. I was sitting in the plane with one of the team members and this lady came on and sat down beside us. She said, "Hi," and we responded, "Hi, how are you?" This started a conversation.

I said, "So, what are you doing here?"

"Well, I was just visiting family. I've gone through a bad divorce..." and so forth.

I said, "We're missionaries; we're on an evangelism team, and we just came back from ministering." Then I asked her about her relationship with God.

She said, "I'm an atheist, and I don't believe in any of that."

I said, "Glory to God, I was raised an atheist! But God's Spirit showed me the Father and showed me the truth."

I began to share with her about the Holy Spirit and how He brought me to Jesus. Her eyes were on me the whole time. Then I began to weep—I mean tears began to pour down my face for this lady. I so wanted her to know the truth.

I said to her, "I want to ask you something. The Holy Ghost told me you would be on this plane today and He wants me to ask you if this plane goes down right now, where would you spend eternity?"

She said, "I never thought of that."

I said, "Because you don't know Jesus as your Savior now, you would go to hell. You don't even know God; He wants you to know Him. It isn't about religion; I'm not here telling you about a religious god; I'm here to tell you about Jesus. He wants you to have a personal relationship with Him."

So, right there, on the plane she gave her heart to Jesus. We gave her some Christian books and she sat and just soaked in those books. When we were ready to leave the plane, she hugged us and said, "Thank you so much; I know that my life is changing already."

I know that God used those tears of compassion to soften her heart and to show her that someone really did care where she would spend eternity.

The Comforter

Tears in her beer

While ministering out on the streets one night, the Holy Spirit drew us to a certain house. We walked up a flight of dark and dingy steps and banged on the door. A young lady came to the door; I peeked over her shoulder and saw a woman sitting on the couch who looked very depressed. The place looked rundown probably due to the depression that this lady was in. She was drinking a beer and there must have been ten empty beer bottles down on the floor beside her.

We told her that the Holy Ghost had sent us and He wanted to minister to her, so they invited us in. It was amazing how those kids, along with their mother, sat and listened so intently to us. They all received Jesus! Then we prayed for the mom who was going through a very rough time and through a very rough relationship with her ex-husband. It had caused her to become depressed. She didn't have a job and she didn't know how she was going to make ends meet either.

It was obvious that God sent us there that night; He knew what she was going through.

About six months later, the next spring we bumped into her on the street. She found a job and looked great; in fact, we didn't even recognize her. She was well groomed and said that her life was a lot better. She remembered what God did for her. Praise God!

Her burden made light

We were heading down to South Minneapolis when all of a sudden I heard in my spirit, "Broadway; go to Broadway." God got our attention in the car and I heard the urgency of His words. As we continued in prayer in the car, I saw in my spirit a house; it was white with green trim and pillars. As we were driving down that street we just happened to look to the left and there it was—the white house with green trim. We prayed for a couple minutes because we wanted to go in at the right time; it's got to be His timing, not our timing. As we got out of the car, three of us went up and a couple stayed in the car praying. We knocked on the door and two guys answered. We told them who we were, and they replied that they were Christians.

Then a woman came to the door and we said to her, "The Holy Ghost has sent us here tonight to minister to you; you need a touch from God."

She asked, "What do you preach?"

"We preach that Jesus is Lord and how He died and rose again for us."

"Oh, come in then."

We shared with her how in prayer God directed us to her house specifically. She was amazed; she looked over at one of the team members and said, "Do you believe this? Do you really believe this?"

He said, "Yeah, of course I do; in prayer I saw the pillars," referring to the pillars in front of her house.

She was so amazed! This lady's husband had just left, so she was able to tell us that she'd had 20 years of a bad marriage with him. He would leave for months and seemed very emotionally unstable. We also found out that she had just been through surgery for a tumor on her brain. When we began to pray with her, God began to give us specific words of knowledge for her that we spoke to her.

She said, "You are so right on; I know God sent you to me!"

We told her that's how much God loved her. God showed up and He wanted her to know that He heard her prayers; He knew she was going through a rough time. It was such a powerful night. We prayed with her and stood in the gap for her marriage. We know that God brought healing that night.

Faithful

From poverty and depression to joy!

The Lord spoke to our hearts about going to South Minneapolis. When we got there we started walking and felt the pulling of the Spirit of God; it was so awesome. It was like He kept pulling us and pulling us down the street to a certain house. Then I stood there and said, "this is the house and this is where God wants us to go." We went up the path and I started to get really excited inside because I knew that the Holy Spirit was going to do something.

All of a sudden through the glass door of the apartment building, we saw this lady we had never met before come running down the stairs. She said to us, "Oh, I'm not the lady you want, you need the lady upstairs; go on up." So we went up and banged on the door and heard, "Come in." There sitting on a two-seater couch, all ripped up and torn, was a sweet young lady in her early thirties. She was very down and depressed.

She was so precious, but she'd been hurt. Her husband had left her so in response she had an affair. Her church had disowned her. She had nothing left except a roof over her head and an old mattress and chair. She had no other furniture, no food, and six little children to take care of.

We ministered to her the love of Jesus; she gave her heart back to Him and got filled with the Holy Ghost. She wept and told us she had been saying, "God, send me help! God, help me!" And God showed up.

The next day we went down and took her bags of groceries so they could eat. After we left, we prayed and asked God to open the door for us to be able to get her some furniture. Two days later, we received a phone call from a man that we knew. He said, "You know, I've got a friend that's got a warehouse full of furniture that he can't use. It's second hand, but it's excellent furniture. Can you use it?"

We picked it up, delivered it to her and were able to furnish her whole apartment. Every single room in her house was furnished! Also, a family brought her brand new bunk beds, and the store donated another set. It just touched my heart that she got everything she needed.

While some of the guys were setting up the furniture, one of her children got ill. They took her to the clinic, and while the mother stayed there with her child, the guys went back at about 6 PM to finish setting up the beds. When they got inside the apartment and the lights were out, they couldn't figure out what was going on. The children had no mattresses on their new beds, but they climbed inside the frame and laid on cushions from the couch and fell asleep. They never ever had their own bed before and God gave them beds!

Also, they didn't know what it was like to sit at a kitchen table and they were so excited they said, "Mommy, can I sit here, can this be my place?"

God heard the cries of that mom; she was His child. Despite what she did, He loved her. He cared for her and He sent us to her at the "midnight hour" when she needed Him the most. God came through for her. We took them to church and had them over for dinner. God wants us not to forsake those that are hurting, but to love them. Thank you Jesus!

Pentecostal dropout returns to the Light

Before we left for Chicago, we were praying for our trip during our team's night of prayer. The Lord revealed to me a prostitute standing under a street light on a corner in Chicago. He said, "She is going to get saved. I'm going to send you down there and I'm going to lead you to her and she's going to know who I am and get set free."

When we got to Chicago we could just feel the Holy Spirit pulling and leading us in the van toward a certain street. We parked the van and walked up the street, and there on the corner, I saw this lady. I asked her about Jesus and she said, "You know, I was raised in a Pentecostal home but I backslid."

"What are you doing now?"

"I'm waiting for a pickup," she said.

I told her the Holy Spirit led us to her and He showed us in prayer that He would bring us to her because she needed to know Him and be set free. That night she came back to Jesus and she said, "Thank you; you saved me tonight." She didn't mean only saving her from hell, but I'm sure she also meant being saved from getting picked up by someone that night.

As we were walking away, one of the people on the team happened to look back and said, "Look! She's was standing under the lamp!" She had been standing underneath the lamp God showed us in prayer. His faithfulness just blows me away!

Wrong number?

God shared with us early in the week that He had someone for us to minister to later that week. We prayed on the day we were supposed to go and the Lord told us He wanted us to go to Lake Street. While we prayed the Lord began to speak to us about this man we were to minister to. He told us that the man felt burned; he was hurting, bitter, and angry with God. He also showed us that it was due to a relationship failure. As we drove down to Lake Street, we saw a guy on a bench on the corner and a couple of us went to talk to him. I stayed in the car while the others went out and ministered. As I sat in the car, I was sensing in my spirit that something was about to happen. I just didn't know what it would be at that time.

All of a sudden, my cell phone rang. "Hello is this so and so?"

I responded, "No."

He said, "I must have the wrong number."

I spoke up and said, "Just a moment; what is your name?" I told him that I was a minister and he said, "Wait a minute; I don't want to go there!" He continued, "I don't have any hope; time is running out; I'm 80 years old today."

I said, "Happy Birthday!" Then I told him everything the Lord showed us about a man that we were to minister to that night. I told him that he was the man and it was no mistake that he called the cell phone that night!

Then he began to share how he had been married twice and had gotten "burned" by them. Then he confessed that he was bitter and mad at God.

I told him, "God is trying to get a hold of you." When I said that, he told me that he has two brothers who are evangelists. I reminded him that it was no accident that he called me that night and it was God that had him call.

He got smart and said, "Why couldn't God give me the right phone number?"

I told him, "You did get the right number; He wanted me to talk to you tonight! God showed us everything that you have gone through, and I was able to tell you all about it tonight."

He replied, "You're right; everything you've spoken is true."

I spoke the word of God that he needed to hear and I know that God got his attention. If God had to make cell phones for just that one call, it would have been worth it!

Little powerhouse

Don't ever underestimate the ability and faith of a child. We had the opportunity to pray for a young Christian boy that was about nine years old. We met him on his porch with the rest of his family. We had a word for him from the Lord, that God wanted to use him in his school to preach the Gospel.

We ended up meeting them again about a half a year later and heard the good news from his mom. She said, "the very next day he shared Jesus with his schoolmates and he hasn't stopped. We told him that Jesus was very proud of him because he put into action what he heard. Praise the Lord!

Hope

How God, how?

All morning I had a stirring to go down to Minneapolis. I wasn't sure when, I wasn't sure why, but I knew that there was something down there for us. Later in prayer, I saw this heavy-set black woman sitting and wondering about something. She was thinking, "God, how are you going to do this? How is this going to happen? I need a miracle." I saw her framework; I saw her face; I knew what she looked like by the Spirit.

We were driving down to South Minneapolis and the Lord said, "I want you to go to Park Avenue." We saw a heavy-set lady go across the road behind us; I felt like I had seen her before. We walked a little way when all of a sudden it felt like the Holy Ghost took my feet and began to pull us. We walked down the block and we saw that lady again and I said, "that's the lady."

I said, "We need to go and pray with her." We went over and started to talk to her and told her the Holy Ghost had sent us to her. I told her I saw in the Spirit her asking God for something.

She believed what I said and responded, "I just got done singing to the Lord, 'bring him to me, bring him to me." We found out she was asking God for a husband. Also, she let us know she wanted more of God in her life.

I told her, "The reason why you're desiring more of God is because God's already got your husband picked out for you—but you're not ready for him. He is already in the ministry and you are needing to get closer to God and grow in Him so that you can line up with what God's got for the two of you." She agreed, then we prayed for her. She knew that God brought her a message of hope. Glory to God!

Lost a daughter but gains new hope.

On a cold a dreary Wednesday afternoon, we went down to North Minneapolis. We felt led of the Lord to go down there. We didn't understand at that time why, but we felt a tugging to go. We got out of the car and seemed to walk forever, passing people up, but had not felt led to talk to them. We kept walking and walking; it seemed like we were at the end of a rope and that the Holy Spirit was ahead pulling us.

We went down a long road and we were passing houses. Suddenly, I said, "We're going to stop at that house, but it's not time yet." After waiting, the Lord said, "Go back."

We went back, knocked on the door and a lady came. She looked very sad. We told her who we were and that the Holy Spirit had sent us to her today. Then we told her that Jesus wanted to touch her.

She said, "I can't talk right now, please, I can't talk."

We said, "Please, let us pray with you; we know that God has sent us to you."

She said, "Look, I've just buried my only daughter today." Then, at that moment, the Lord touched her and she invited us to come in to her house.

We were able to give her new hope. We said, "You know, Jesus loves you so much." She received Jesus that day, and she received the hope that she would see her daughter again. That was so awesome that Jesus sent us to her during her time of grief. It was an awesome time of ministry that we will never forget. God is so good.

Power

From the mire to Holy Ghost Fire

We went on a short mission trip to Milwaukee with an evangelism team. Before going out we prayed, "God, where do you want us to be today?" He led us to a certain street where we heard a lady talking from a far way off.

As we approached her she continued to be loud and a bit obnoxious as she asked us, "What do you guys got there?" It was obvious she had been drinking as we handed her a tract.

I said, "Do you know, if you were to die today, would you go to heaven?"

She responded, "I've already been there."

"What do you mean, you've already been to heaven?"

"I died on the operating table. Right now, I'm living with a pig's valve in my heart."

It didn't make any difference to us whether she said she'd been to heaven or not. She was backslidden, and there were things going on in her life that she didn't want to share. But the Holy Spirit always reveals the truth! We talked to her, and the Lord spoke through us to her and it brought conviction.

Then He wanted us to pray with her, so she could give her heart back to Jesus. She repented, and she said that ever since she had died and came back, she went the wrong way. She went the way of the world, and was using alcohol and drugs. She had the attitude, "Well, I've gone and seen heaven, and I know I'm okay." But truly, that was not the case—she was not okay. She thought just because she was once saved, she would always be saved.

We prayed for deliverance from alcohol and drugs. I'm telling you, the power of God was so strong neither of us could hardly stand up. The anointing came upon her; and the Word of God says that the anointing destroys the yolk and it removes the burden (See Isaiah 10:27). The Holy Spirit destroyed the yolk of the bondage to alcohol and drugs that was on her that day.

We could also see her heart had been hurt and wounded. The Holy Spirit spoke a word through us to her, and encouraged her.

Then I said to her, "You have got such a powerful testimony. Now you've been set free from alcohol and drugs and God is going to be glorified through this." Then I said, "You need to share what God has done for you today. You know what? I see you, one day, standing behind a pulpit sharing this powerful testimony of what God has done and how God saved you from death and from the things of this world."

She said, "My dad is a Pastor and he told me, 'when you're ready, I want you to come and stand up in front of the church, and share about what God has done for you.'"

That was a confirmation for her that day! Before we left, she wanted some of our tracts, so we gave her some. She immediately went out and started handing them out and talking to people! It was obvious that God absolutely turned her around.

So you see, just because someone says, "I've been to heaven," doesn't mean that it's where they're going to end up.

Jesus passes by

We had the privilege this last spring to go on a short mission trip to Mexico City. On the first day we needed to go to the store to buy some supplies for the outreach we would be doing. We got quite a few things and we all thought that we should get a cab to take us home. When we arrived at the house and were about to step out of the old Volkswagen Bug cab, we saw an ambulance and police car go by very fast. They stopped about six houses down from where we were. We heard a dog barking and a crowd of people gathering.

We went down there and saw a lady lying in a pool of blood. Her elderly mother was there; she was shaking so much and was so scared. We found out that her daughter had fallen from three stories high. There was blood everywhere, her chest and arms were swollen. Two of the team members went up with the mother into her house and began to comfort her because she was in shock.

Meanwhile the Lord told me to keep pressing in and pray the whole time in the Holy Ghost. The next thing I knew I was standing beside her and the policeman said, "We need your help." So I began to undo bandages and rip tape. The Lord gave me a scripture as I stood there from Ezekiel 16:6: "And when I passed by you and saw you struggling in your own blood, I said to you in your blood, 'Live!' Yes, I said to you in your blood 'Live.'"

I began to speak that scripture over her again and again and continued to pray in the Holy Ghost.

The two other team members came down and I said to the one that spoke Spanish, "Please go to the ambulance and tell her that Jesus loves her."

As the ambulance began to leave, everyone who was standing there from the block prayed for her fervently. The power of God was evident as we prayed.

About a week later I was meditating upon the scripture the Lord gave me from Ezekiel. The Lord spoke this to my heart, "When you walked by her that day and saw her struggling in her own blood, it was I who passed by her and it was I who was speaking life into her that day through you."

We just found out on the last trip to Mexico that this woman's health is wonderful with no damage from the fall she had. Praise God!

New Wine for a wino

We went to a cell group meeting in Mexico City to minister. It was in a tiny room but the power of God was strong. After we were done ministering the Word of God, a man came into the room who was stone drunk. I mean, he was out of it and he kept babbling to us and could barely stand. We knew he needed Jesus and he needed to be delivered.

We shared with him about Jesus and I know what some people thought, "How can you talk to someone who is drunk?" Well, it's with the *heart* that we believe, so we ministered to him about Jesus. He received Jesus as his Lord and then we prayed for him to be delivered from this spirit of alcohol. We laid hands on him and the power of God just went through this man. He wasn't totally sober at first, but he was drying up.

Then the compassion of God came upon us and we began to really love on him. We knew it was Jesus' love. I told someone to go and get him some coffee and a chair. All of a sudden, I started to sing *"Amazing Grace"* and this man began to sing with us. His heart was being moved as he sang.

Since then we have heard from the pastor of the cell group that he is doing wonderful. He is going to his church and participates on their evangelism team. He has stayed sober for about five months and has kept a job. Also, we recently found out that he has met a Christian woman and is engaged to be married.

Demons out of Deborah

I would like to let you know that even today, God does make house calls. In prayer, we sensed the leading of the Holy Spirit to a particular block in the south Minneapolis area. As we drove down that block, we looked to the left and saw some people on a porch. Glory to God; we knew in our heart that those were the people the Lord wanted us to minister to. We went up on to the porch and told them the Holy Ghost sent us. There was no "fireworks" at first, but we just kept on talking to them while being sensitive to the Holy Spirit.

A woman and her daughter lived at the house. We ended up talking to the daughter first; she was in a backslidden condition. We ministered and prayed for her and had a word of knowledge for her. We told her that she had a desire to work with youth.

We found out later that she told her mom, "Those people had to be sent by God because no one knew that." So, the word of knowledge is a powerful gift out in the streets.

After we prayed for her, her mother asked, "Can you pray for me, too?"

"Yeah, we can pray for you too."

We stepped inside the foyer of their house and the Holy Ghost was very present as we began to pray. All of a sudden, we looked at her and her face was kind of contorted and she didn't look very happy. We've seen that look before—it was demons.

She loved the Lord, but as a child her father was a Satanist high priest. He had committed her to Satan, made her drink blood and raped her. She went through some awful things and a door was opened to many demonic spirits early on in her life. So, we cast those demons out, right there. Glory to God! God really ministered to her.

We met her later that year at a church we were visiting. She told us how God continued to work in her that whole night. She said she was shaking all night and when she asked the Lord what He was doing, He said, "I'm purging you." Glory to God; He is into the restoration business!

Drawn by the Father

We were in prayer one Thursday afternoon on a cold winter day. The Lord told us that there was a prodigal son who wanted to come home, and when he returns he would be drawn to us like a magnet. I saw this big magnet in my spirit; we knew we would be like magnets because of the Holy Spirit in us.

The Holy Spirit took us down to the Greyhound bus station in downtown Minneapolis.

While we were ministering to a man who was on parole for murder, we noticed another man peek his head out from around the corner. All of a sudden, he came running up toward us shouting, "Please pray for me; I'm a sinner! I have sinned today! I've fallen away from God, please help me!"

He was drawn to us just like a magnet, grabbing our hands and hanging on to us. We prayed with him and he gave his life back to the Lord! Then we prayed for the Lord to give him direction. It fulfilled the word that the Lord showed us during prayer—the prodigal came home that night! Glory to God!

The Loving Rebuker

Smile! You're on God's camera!

One night in October, the Lord told us to go to a bar in North Minneapolis. I thought, "A bar, Lord? You wouldn't have me go into a bar." Sure enough, he did. I remember several dreams I have had where I've gone into a bar, ordered a Coke and somebody got saved.

God told us exactly what bar to go to and what time we needed to go. We got in the car and we were praying and the Holy Spirit said, "She's going to be a white woman, blonde hair, and I want you to ask her one question from Me: 'What are you doing here?'"

The bar was really smoky and there was a lot of cussing going on. The bartender said, "What do you want to drink?" I ordered a coke, even though I don't drink coke. We sat there for a few minutes, praying quietly to ourselves, waiting on the Holy Spirit. I looked over in the other room (which was the billiard room) and I saw a white woman with blonde hair. The Lord said, "That's the lady. I want you to go over and minister to her."

We went over and introduced ourselves. I told her, "The Holy Ghost sent us down here tonight to find you."

I said, "Do you believe that the Lord sent us down here?"

She said, "Yes."

I said, "Do you know for sure that if you were to die tonight that you would go to heaven?"

She said, "yes" again.

"How do you know?"

"I'm a born-again Christian. Jesus has come into my heart and forgiven me of my sins."

I said, "I have one question for you from the Holy Ghost. He wants to know what are you doing here?"

Isn't that powerful?! Right there and then, we got to minister to her. We told her that God had so much more for her and that He knew exactly where she was at. He knew what she was doing, and He wanted her to be aware of that. She confessed to be a Christian; that's why God wanted to ask her, "What are you doing here?"

It's like if you were doing something and not knowing that somebody could see you. Then they point out the security camera to you. It was like she was doing all these things without realizing that God was in that bar and could see her. We pointed out that she was on "God's Candid Camera." God did see where she was and what she was doing. It brought conviction knowing this, and that's what God wanted to do! God had us do it in a way that she would still know that He loved her.

Back on track

While in prayer, the Lord showed us in our spirit a yellow house with a young man in rebellion standing on the porch. Because the Lord showed us this, we were able to pray specifically for the situation and bind and uproot the spirit of rebellion before we got there. This prepared the way for us to accomplish what God had for us that night.

When we got to the house we zeroed in on the young man the Lord showed us in our spirit. We found out that he was —well, he *confessed* to be a Christian.

We shared with him how God had shown us in prayer a man in rebellion at a yellow house standing on the front porch. As we ministered to him, he kept saying, "Yeah. I know the Lord," but there was hesitancy in his voice. We knew he wasn't telling us the whole truth.

As we continued to speak what was on our heart, he confessed he was using marijuana. Then such soberness came over him and he asked, "What do I need to do?" His attitude changed; he was so awestruck by the fact that God had come to visit him through us. We gave him the uncompromised Gospel: you need to lose your life to Jesus so you'll truly have your life. He didn't care about the others who were around; he prayed with us to give his life totally to the Lord.

Because we brought him that specific information, it caused him to see that God was always watching him and nothing can be hidden from Him.

Free at last!

While in prayer, the Lord showed us that we needed to go down to North Minneapolis on Lyndale Avenue where we would meet a man in his 30's. So, we went down there and just as the Holy Spirit had said, we saw the man on the corner as we drove by. We stopped him and said "The Holy Ghost has sent us to you." We told him how God showed him to us in our spirit before we got there.

We then spoke the word that the Lord gave us for him; it was a strong word. Even though this guy was gentle, his heart was quite hard. When we saw him he had just come from the liquor store and had a bottle wrapped in a paper bag in his hand.

He told us, "I'm not ready to come to the Lord right now; I'm going to come to Him when I'm ready." Somehow the devil had conned him into thinking that was honorable. He thought he could just live the life of sin because at least he wasn't coming to God being a hypocrite.

We said, "Is the pleasure of your sin worth eternity in Hell? You can't be playing games with your life." We went on to say, "The end could come and you're not ready." Then we told him how God is patient, not willing that any should perish, but that all should come to repentance (See 2 Peter 3:9).

At that point when he was ready to say goodbye, the Holy Spirit spoke to my heart, "Don't let him go; I want him to know Me."

I said to him, "I can't let you go without you knowing who Jesus is." I continued to minister to him about who Jesus really was and said, "Let's pray." I reached out for his hand and he gave me his hand to pray. I'm telling you, you could just see his heart melt at that time as he invited Jesus into his heart. He asked Him to be his Savior and his Lord.

Then I asked him, "What kind of need do you have?"

He said, "Oh, it's funny that you should ask that. I have just come out of a shelter three days ago with my girlfriend and three children. We just got a little apartment and we need everything."

God laid it on our heart to help him the best we could. We were able to furnish their apartment and bring them bags of food. They were totally blessed.

When we went down there the next day, his girlfriend spoke to me and said, "He proposed to me! He asked me to marry him last night." We were really excited about that because it showed that he took his new walk with Jesus seriously. Then she said, "He came home a totally different person last night; he was happy and had joy."

We said, "It's because he had a visit from the Holy Ghost."

Bar stool to church pew

We went to Chicago to be part of a vigil that commemorated the death of a Pastor's son we knew. While there, God led us to an area about a mile from the church. We met a man who was on his way home from the bar and he had a bottle in his hand.

He said, "I guess you just got me in time."

As we talked to him, we could tell that he knew the Holy Ghost had sent us. When we told him that there needed to be a change, he really agreed. He shared how at one time, he knew the Lord but had backslid and had gotten into a bad rut he couldn't get out of. We prayed for him and cursed the addictions that controlled his life. We then invited him down to the church service going on that night and he said, "I'll be there." We didn't doubt that he would be there; this was a divine appointment.

He came that night with his girlfriend and sat on the back row. He went forward for the altar call they had that night to totally give his life over to Jesus. The Lord touched and changed him that very night. It's awesome to see how God works things together! Praise the Lord!

Sidewalk altar

One night we were drawn to a specific street in St. Paul where a lady crossed our path. We ministered to her and asked her if she knew Jesus. She told us that she once had a relationship with the Lord. While she was sharing her past, a conviction began to come over her. Without us rebuking her, she began to confess her sins and admit that she had backslidden. She told us how before she had been going to church and living for the Lord, but during that time she was befriended by the wrong people. She started drinking with them and fell away from the Lord.

As we continued to listen to her, she took her cigarettes out of her pocket and she stomped on them. She fell to her knees weeping, not caring who was passing by. She cried out to God for forgiveness.

She needed that direct appointment from the Holy Ghost at that time. She knew that the Holy Ghost had sent us to her that night. We prayed for her to be set free from the bondages in her life, and the Lord did indeed set her FREE!

Truth

Drawn to a true witness

We were in prayer when God told us an exact location in the city we needed to go to. He said, "Someone is going to come up to you and look at you straight face to face and say, 'what are you doing?'"

When we got to the area, one of the team members went to witness to a guy that was by a bus stop. At first the gentleman didn't want to listen. He walked away from the team member, and then he came face to face with me and said, "What are you doing?"

I told him, "I'm here preaching the good news," and he told me he was a Jehovah's Witness. I began to minister to him the word of God and he listened very intently. He ended up getting saved that night; it was so awesome! He said he was drawn to me; I know that it was the Spirit of God!

Two

Train'n Ground

You may be asking yourself, "Can I do this? Can I be a bold witness?" You were not called to do anything in your own strength, power, or ability. So the answer is, yes, you can, do all things through Christ who strengthens you" (Philippines 4:13)!

The following testimonies will show you the areas in which we grew while in training. There were a few times of questioning and hesitation. We pray that these testimonies will help you to be more aware of the leading of the Holy Spirit in your own life.

God's love shows through a runny nose & frozen toes!

We were in prayer one really cold Thursday afternoon. It was the middle of winter and the forecast was for 21 degrees below zero. The Lord spoke to my heart and said, "I want you to go down to a hospital tonight. Go into the back of the hospital because there will be sitting on the steps a man and a woman waiting for you. The man is hurting and he's going to need a touch from Me; I want you to go to them."

I said, "That can't be you, Lord, it's too cold." But he kept nudging me, and so I said, "I don't know if this is God or not, but I keep on hearing, 'Go to a hospital.'"

"What hospital are we to go to?"

"I don't know, but it's in Minneapolis. I see it in my spirit; I know what it looks like. In the back there's some steps, and we need to go there."

We prayed, and then we knew we needed to go.

We got really bundled up; I had so many layers of clothes on. When we got downtown we decided to park in the general vicinity of a certain hospital. We got out and were frozen after only having walked a little way. We saw a light on in a building across the street.

I said, "I've got to get out of this cold —I'm freezing."

So we went into the building across the street and met a security guard. He said, "What are you guys doing out here on a night like this?"

"Well, we're trying to find a hospital."

"What hospital?"

Its' name just came to us and we told him.

The security guard said, "I'll tell you what, If you go up these steps here, through the corridors, down the hallway and through a tunnel, it will take you to a hospital. Maybe that's what you're looking for."

We came to the top of a flight of steps and we saw two people, a man and a woman, at the bottom. It was so powerful! I knew right then and there it was them! We went down the steps and I tried to break the ice by saying, "Hi, it's cold; what are you two doing out here?"

The lady said, "Well, his mom is on her last breath and he's having a very, very difficult time; he loves his mom."

I said, "Well, you know what? The Holy Ghost sent us to you tonight. He told us that we would find you at the bottom of some steps!"

At first, the guy didn't want to hear from us. His girlfriend said to him, "You'd better listen to them because the Holy Ghost sent them to you. God sent them to you; you'd better listen."

So we began to share with him the love of Jesus. He received Jesus and then we prayed for him and his mom. We prayed that he would have peace in his heart. It was such a powerful time of ministry to him. Then he stood up; took both of us in his arms and said, "Thank you, thank you so much for coming! I know I'm going to be all right now."

Then they left and he went into the hospital to say their last goodbye to his mom. That was a powerful night. It was vitally important that we arrived at the hospital the way we did. The Lord even used the cold to get us into the right door; truly God led our steps.

When we left I said, "You know, Lord, I'm sorry. I'm sorry that I questioned You when you told me to go out in this cold." The Lord spoke to my heart, "I didn't ask you to go to the cross, I just asked you to go out in the cold to minister to someone who was hurting." Ever since that day I have tried to be sensitive and do what He has asked me to do.

Worth the wait

As I look at what the Holy Spirit has done in my life, I realize that there was a starting point. There was a time where I was stretched to believe what God wanted to bring me into. It took patience and perseverance to hang on to the vision God gave me.

I remember it so well; it was like yesterday. I was two years old in the Lord and just newly baptized in the Holy Spirit when the Lord spoke to my heart that He was going to send me to Africa. I said, "me Lord?" I had no desire to leave home, much less go to Africa.

He continued by showing me a vision in my spirit of a village. I saw a little mud hut with smoke coming out of the door; standing by the door was a witch doctor. I also saw an old broken down stall with a cow tied to it. Then He said, "everyone in the village will get saved, including the witch doctor."

Something happened that day that would change my life forever. I started a journey—not really knowing what I was getting into, but having a peace that someday God would send me to Africa. For twenty-one years I had the same vision on a continuous basis. God showed it to me, it seemed like, all the time.

All those years, it would have been easy to give up on the vision, but I knew I couldn't. The enemy would try to discourage me by saying things like, *"Why would He choose you? You're not a missionary, and look at how long it's been."* But, I chose to keep on believing what the Lord had said and shown me.

Twenty years after I first saw the vision, my daughter went to India. When I went to see her off after her training in New York, the Lord spoke to me and said, "I want you to take a youth team to Africa next year." So I went home and prepared a team and myself to leave.

The Lord took us to Tanzania in East Africa. While there, He led us into the bush where I saw a village with: a hut with smoke coming out of the door, a stall with a cow tied to it, and yes, a witch doctor. When we were done ministering, it was just like the Holy Spirit had shown me; the village and the witch doctor got saved.

Later I asked the Lord, "Why did I need to wait so long?" He replied, "The team was not even born yet; you prayed for your team for twenty-one years." I can now say it was worth the wait.

Oh no, not me Lord!

Several years ago I had an opportunity to go home to England to see my mother. Growing up in England, I lived beside a lady named Mrs. Boraham who always made remarks at the way I dressed. I used to wear short mini skirts and I'm sure she used to think some terrible things about me. I really didn't care at the time, I thought that she was such an old fuddy-duddy.

During my visit, while I was riding my bike running an errand for my mom, I sensed in my spirit that I needed to visit Mrs. Boraham. I just sensed such a leading of the Holy Spirit to go up to see her at the little bungalow up in the village she had moved into. I knew her husband had died and she could not take care of herself very well. The Holy Spirit was really moving on me to go up and see her.

I thought, "Lord, You know what she thinks about me." Also at that time, I really didn't feel I had the boldness that was required to talk to her, but I kept feeling this prompting that just wouldn't go away.

So, I finally went up to talk to her. I knocked on the door and I heard, "Come on in." She was sitting on the couch so I sat down to talk to her for a little while. I began to share with her about what the Lord had done in my life. She was totally astonished about the change that had taken place in me from the time that I had seen her last. She could not believe what God had done for me because I had been a young girl with a lot of problems. I had an abusive father and I sought after love in all the wrong places.

As I began to share, she could not believe the knowledge and faith that I had in Christ. She made the point that I knew more of the Word of God than the Vicar of the church in the village. I continued to share with her about God's love and what He did for her and asked her if she would like to receive Jesus as her personal Savior. She received Him that day and she was so touched. I prayed with her some more and we said our good-byes. The Lord knew that being a faithful churchgoer was not enough. He knew that her time was really near and how important it was that she knew who He was. I knew the Holy Spirit ordered my steps there that day, because a week later she died. Oh, I thank you Lord; I thank you Jesus!

It really has made me realize that if I had not heeded to the prompting of the Holy Spirit she could have gone to eternal Hell. So, I pray that God will always help me to heed His voice.

Three

God's Timing

It's not just what you do, it's also when you do it. Timing is so very important because it can mean life or death to someone. You may be at the right place, but you have to be there at the right time if you're going to meet that right person. If God says to you, "I want you there at 9 PM," you need to be there at 9 PM. It is important to get the perfect timing of God, because if you're a minute late someone could miss out on a miracle.

Breath of Life

Here's an awesome testimony of God's delivering and saving power, and the split second accuracy that the Holy Spirit will give us.

God brought us down to HCMC (Hennepin County Medical Center) on a Wednesday at 11 AM. That's the time that we felt in our heart that we needed to go down to visit a man from church. He had an abscessed tooth, and the infection went to his heart and he went into a coma. He was on life support the Sunday that they announced it at church.

We went down Wednesday and found him sitting up, drinking water and talking a little bit; God had already done an awesome miracle. We were able to pray for him and encourage him.

When we got outside, and crossed the first intersection from the hospital, the Holy Spirit caused me to look back over my shoulder. I saw a girl I knew with her mother waiting in their car at the intersection. We waved them over to talk to them. We found out that the girl's cousin had a drug overdose from crack cocaine. This cousin's mother had found him in the basement gasping for air that morning. They didn't know how long he had been alone like that, but she called the ambulance as soon as she found him.

God showed us that we should go back at 6 PM that night to visit him, as he lay in a coma in Intensive Care.

We prayed going down there and the Holy Ghost filled us up for what was coming. We found out where he was and went up to his room. There was no one else in the room when we arrived; the family had just gone to get a bite to eat.

We began to pray for him and speak words of life over him that he was healed! When believers lay hands on the sick, they do recover! We then shared about Jesus with him and prayed a simple prayer that we knew he heard even though he was in a coma. There was such a wonderful presence of the Lord as we prayed.

We were there ministering to him for about 20 minutes when his mother came up and we introduced ourselves. We had an opportunity to encourage her and instruct her in speaking the Word of God over her son. We told her it was vitally important what she says concerning the outcome of her son.

His mother said, "Tell him that when he wakes up not to take the respirator tube out of his mouth." We were, needless to say, a lot more relaxed than the family, who seemed somber. So, I just started to say while giggling a bit, "Listen here, don't spit the tube out. I remember when I had tubes in my mouth when I was sick. If you spit them out, they just shove them back in. You spit them out, they put it back in again." Then the man who was in a coma began to laugh—

not out loud, he was too weak, but for a man that was in a coma it was a miracle!

We have received word that he has gotten out of the hospital and is doing well. Praise the Lord!

Right on schedule

March the 8th, was the original date I wanted to go down to Florida to see my daughter who was training to go on a mission trip. I checked the flights and found out the only seats available were extremely expensive. I knew that the Holy Spirit had called me to go so I checked my frequent flyer miles and found out I had just enough to get a ticket with them. When I called to redeem my miles for a ticket they said they were full in regular class but they would give me a first class seat instead. The only catch was, I couldn't go on the 8th—they only had a seat for me on the 7th. I decided that I would take it; I knew that the Lord was in it.

I boarded the flight and a man sat down beside me as I read my book. Then the Lord spoke to me and said, "I want you to talk to that man sitting beside you." I asked him who he was, and if his trip to Florida was for business or a vacation. He told me his name and that he was the vice president of a big corporation. He continued to tell me that he was going down to meet his wife and son who had flown down earlier that week. I began to talk to him about my life and testimony and what the Lord had done for me.

He said, "My wife is a wonderful Christian woman, but I have an interest in Buddhism." He proceeded to tell me that he had been married for eighteen years, but ten years ago his marriage came to a standstill after his son was born. He then told me about a woman he worked with that he was attracted to. He told me he had never had an affair with her but he was definitely attracted to this woman.

I told him, "if you lust after her with your eyes, it's as if you are committing adultery according to the bible."

He agreed, and told me he was raised in a Catholic home and had been educated in a Catholic school. He did have some understanding of who God was, but definitely didn't have a personal relationship with Jesus. He said, "I don't know why I'm telling you all this; I'm just spilling my guts out to you."

I said, "Because God wants you to know that what you're doing is wrong and he put me here beside you today to tell you."

Then he told me he has a close acquaintance that was coming to Minneapolis soon – the Dalai Lama.

I said, "Oh yeah, I heard about that from my daughter about a week ago; I'm praying against that."

"Why."

"Do you know what he is doing?"

"Yeah, he is going to be playing with sand then throwing it into the river."

I responded, "He is going to be doing more than playing with sand. He is going to be doing sand art, throwing it into the river, then calling forth seven hundred demons into the city." The look on his face was pure terror when I said this.

He said, "What? He didn't tell me that; he didn't tell me that is what he was going to do! What do you mean he's going to be calling forth seven hundred demons into the city?"

I said, "Do you think that the devil is going to tell you the truth? The devil tries to kill, steal, and destroy, and he has already started on your family."

He said, "I'm going to look into this."

I said, "You're going to go to your friend, and do you think he is going to tell you the truth? He's not going to tell you the truth—the devil NEVER tells you the truth! You need to know Jesus so that you can know the truth and He will be able to show you right from wrong. The only way that you will know the truth is from God." That day God really worked on his heart.

Then he told me that he had missed two flights that day. The first one he missed by twelve minutes, and the second he missed as a standby passenger. I told him, "it's no mistake that you are on this flight; God had a purpose and that was for you to sit beside me and hear the truth."

Lost and found

Several years ago I worked in a nursing home. One day, toward the end of my shift, I noticed a little lady that I just loved who was wandering trying to find her room. I sensed in my heart the Lord telling me to go up and talk to her and show her where to go.

"What's the matter?" I said.

"I'm lost. I don't know where my room is."

"You know where your room is; you've never been lost before." Then I said, "your room's down there," as I pointed.

Then the Holy Spirit said, "No, I want you to take her down there; I have something for you to do in there." So I took her to her room, got her all settled and made sure she was peaceful.

Then I heard, coming from the other side of the curtain that divided the room, breathing that was very labored and heavy. I went behind the curtain and there was a lady on a respirator in a coma. She looked like she was just about ready to die.

I pulled up a chair, took her hand and started talking to her. I know when you're in a coma you can hear what other people are saying to you, so I began to talk to her about Jesus.

I said, "You know Gladys, Jesus is getting ready to come for you, but you need to make sure your heart is right first. He wants you to go to heaven, so I'm going to pray with you and if you believe what I'm saying to you, I want you to squeeze my hand or just let me know that you believe in what I'm saying."

I prayed with her to receive Jesus and as I began to pray, tears began to trickle down her face. I knew that she had heard and received Jesus that day. Then I gave her a kiss on the forehead and I told her I would see her in heaven some day. About four hours later, Gladys went home to be with Jesus.

Miracle on 7th Avenue

I was worshipping the Lord on a Saturday morning when the Lord spoke to my heart and said, "I want you to go down to 7th Avenue in South Minneapolis at two in the morning." It was a cold and windy day; my first thought was that I didn't want to go out in this cold tonight, but we knew we needed to go!

We arrived in south Minneapolis just a couple minutes before two AM and drove slowly down 7th Avenue. A couple of drug dealers started to approach our van, but then backed away. We went around the block and ended up back on 7th Avenue and the Lord said, "park here on the corner." We didn't see any sign of life as we parked, but we knew the Lord is always faithful and on time. The street looked dark and desolate. In front of us was a car, but we didn't see anyone in it at first. Then, after a moment, we saw a flicker of light come from inside the car. The Lord said, "that's the one."

The Lord had showed us in prayer that day what we would be facing. He told us that this person was "drowning and sinking fast." We sensed she knew the Lord at one time, but had chosen the way of the world. The Lord showed me in my spirit an apple with a worm in it. This represented sin and rottenness in her life. We also heard the words, "healing anointing," but didn't know what that meant for this situation at the time. There was a real excitement in our spirit that God was going to change someone's life that night!

We went over to the car and found out that there were two women sitting in it. We asked them their names, what they where up to, and if they where Christians. The one in the passenger side responded roughly, "yea, I go to church." We told them the Holy Spirit had sent us down there for a reason. The lady in the passenger seat told us that they where pressed for time but we continued to search for the reason the Lord had sent us. We asked them if they needed prayer for anything. The lady in the driver seat said, "I need God to change me;" at that moment, the other lady left the car. As one of us began to pray for her, I heard the words, "holiness and sanctification" in my spirit. I told her, "you need to pray, but its going to take some action and decisions on your part for this change to come. You need to come out of the way this world does things, and follow the Lord. It will mean that you will lose some friends and the world will not appreciate how you live. Some will ridicule you, but it's a decision you need to make." Leaning over to her, I told her that the Lord had showed us that she had a relationship with Him at one time. Despite the decisions she made, God loved her so much that He came to visit her through us at 2 AM that night.

I laid my hands on her and asked the Lord to fill her up again with His Spirit. I saw a river flowing out of her. The Lord spoke through me, "There's a healing anointing flowing out of you like a river and God wants to take that gift of healing in you and use it to heal others." She began to weep as I said this. She knew this was true and that she had a call on her life.

Jesus came to restore her and give her another chance. She told us before we left, "I know where I'm going tomorrow—back to church." We praise God that He pulled her out of a pit that night and caused her to see clearly again.

Right place, right time

Around 10 PM the Lord said, "It's time; I want you to leave." So, we got in the car and drove where He led us. We went to an area in the city, parked our car and then walked up and down a specific street. We knew we needed to be at the right place at the right time.

As we were approaching a car with a lady sitting in the passenger seat, we saw a man come down the steps of a house. We went over to talk to him as he began to look under the hood of the car. We talked to him and found out he didn't have a personal relationship with the Lord.

God set him free that night as he gave his life to the Lord Jesus. He knew that the Holy Ghost sent us to him. Then I went over to the front of the car and talked to the lady inside. She said, "I'm his aunt; I've been praying for him for a long time; praise God!"

So it really doesn't matter what time of the day or night it is, God will have you right there at the right time. Praise God!

Scared to life!

After being instructed by the Holy Spirit, we went to stand in front of a bar in North Minneapolis. He told us to go down to the bar at precisely 11 PM. Quite a few people passed us by but God didn't want us to stop any of them. Then came a gentleman down the sidewalk—"I think that's the guy." As he walked towards us, we began to talk to him. About minute later, we heard a gunshot inside the bar. BOOM! A lady came flying out of the front door saying, "Someone's been shot in there!"

The guy we were talking to started to walk away quickly. We followed him and we weren't going to let him get away. We knew that God had called us down there for him. He was afraid and said, "I've got to get out of here." So, we walked down to the end of the block with him and stopped. We continued to talk to him and give him the Gospel. Right there, he repented and he got his life right with Jesus and he confessed Jesus as his Lord! Then He told us he was excited to get back to church.

God used this situation of somebody getting shot to get through to this man. I'm sure it caused him to realize how short life is.

After the man got saved, we began to pray for the person who was shot inside. God spoke to us and said, "There is some momma praying for her boy in there." God also brought us down there to pray for that man and be on-site prayer warriors.

Put 'em up...and praise the Lord!

We had just gotten done with evangelism class and it was pretty late at night, but God sent us down to Minneapolis to minister anyway. God led us to park at a Target store where we would meet our divine appointment.

Suddenly, I turned my head and saw a guy swaying so bad, walking across the parking lot. He looked drunk and was a total mess. Out of my mouth came, "Oh, he needs Jesus!"

I said to him, "Hey, man, what's up?"

He said, "You don't want to know."

I started to talk to him about Jesus anyway, and he said, "Oh, God can't forgive me."

"Why can't He forgive you?"

"Because you don't know what I just did."

"What did you just do?"

"I just went into a big department store, and stole a lot of stuff. I was just about ready to go into Target and steal some more stuff, but you stopped me."

"No, I didn't stop you, but the Holy Ghost stopped you because He loves you."

We ministered to him and I led him to Jesus, but he still couldn't forgive himself.

I said, "You've got to forgive yourself and then take the stuff back that you stole."

He said, "I'm going to. I already made the decision after you talked to me about Jesus. That's what I need to do."

But God wasn't done with him yet. We prayed for his deliverance from alcohol. Here was a man that was totally drunk—totally. He was completely sober by the time we got done praying with him. He talked sober, he walked sober, he was thinking sober. He was totally delivered! What was so awesome was he kept wanting us to pray, so we prayed for the baptism of the Holy Spirit. The Spirit of God just flowed out of him like a river. He got his prayer language. It was an awesome miracle of God done in him that night.

Then we had a revival party right in the parking lot. It was so awesome! We began to dance, praise God and just rejoice in seeing the deliverance of this man. He was about ready to make another mistake, but God stopped him. We praise God for this awesome deliverance!

Angels of mercy

We were in prayer crying out to God for doors to be opened and, in my spirit, He showed me a big door. Then a young man who was praying with us said, "I don't know if you're going to believe this or not; I saw an angel kneeling down where you were at, and as you were praying and speaking, the angel was listening."

God showed me that the angel was waiting to receive instructions from my prayers to move out on my behalf. I was so excited!

The Lord had us go to a certain house; we knocked and the man who opened the door said, "Oh, we're not interested, there's a lot going on here tonight and you don't want to know about it. I don't have time to talk to you, so I'd appreciate it if you'd just leave." Then he tried to convince us that there wasn't anyone else in the house and that he was getting ready to leave. I knew in my spirit that there was a lady in the house that God wanted us to minister to. However, I sensed we needed to leave at that time. I knew that we would be led back there before the night was over.

So we left and the Lord said, "Keep walking." We went across the street. He said, "I want you to go to the very end of this road; I want you to cross the street, then I want you to turn around and go back to the house." We did just as the Lord said, and as we were walking back we saw in the distance a couple of guys leave the house and drive away in a car. The Lord said, "Now, I want you to go back."

I knocked on the door and heard, "Come on in." The lady didn't open the door; she just called us to come in not even knowing who we were. We went into the kitchen and met a woman and her daughter. You could tell the oppression was so bad and so deep. We began to minister to her and told her that the Holy Ghost specifically called us to her house that night; He knew what she was going through and what was happening to her.

We prayed with her about her abusive situation and she wept as God ministered to her and brought her a new hope. God broke through the walls of oppression that night. We serve an awesome God!

So, when someone says, "No," we need to be sensitive to the timing of God. Even though at first it wasn't the right time to come in, we knew God led us there for a reason.

Four

His Leading

The leading of the Holy Spirit will always produce good fruit. The bible says, "the steps of a good man are ordered by the Lord, and He delights in his way"(Psalm 37:23). You have to trust that as you are being led by Him, He will lead you where you need to go.

When the disciples came back from preaching the Gospel, Jesus rejoiced and said, "I thank you Father…that you have hidden these things from the wise and prudent and revealed them to babes"(Luke 10:21). The truth was hidden from the "know-it-alls," but was revealed to those who simply trusted their Father. So, let's be "simple" and follow the Holy Spirit, as we trust Him.

Here are some testimonies where His leadership produced good fruit.

God is always opening doors

One Thursday evening God spoke to our hearts and told us He would be sending us to North Minneapolis to a white house with green trim. He said the door would be open for me to minister. I did not understand that at the time He meant the door would be literally open.

As the team and I began to minister on the streets, we felt drawn to walk up Broadway Avenue. All of a sudden, I felt like the Holy Spirit turned my head to the left and I noticed a long, dark side road with no lights. Across the street in the alley I saw some guys dealing drugs. The Holy Spirit said, "This is the street. I want you to walk down this way; this is where the house is."

We walked about three houses down and to my left I saw it; I knew it was the house. The door was wide open on a winter's night! I knew it was an invitation to go in and minister.

We rang the bell but no one came so I proceeded up the steps with the team behind me. I called to see if anyone was in the house and I noticed at the top of the stairs a lot of boots, coats and hats. I called one more time and no one came.

Then I said, "Lord, I know that this is the place; this is the house; this is the door that you led me to." No sooner had I said that, a man appeared at the top of the steps and said with a gruff voice, "What do you want?" I told him my name and where I was from. I told him that the Holy Spirit had led me to his house to minister to him.

We talked to him and he received what I had to say; he received Jesus as his Lord and Savior. As it was time for us to go, he took my hand and smiled and said, "God bless you."

I told him that the Holy Spirit led us there, because he needed to recognize the power of the Holy Spirit. I knew there was going to be a situation in his life where he would need to know that the Holy Spirit knew where he was at.

God knows your business

On a Wednesday evening a friend of ours spoke to us and told us of a conversation he had with one of the servers while having breakfast a Denny's. He ministered to her and realized that she needed a woman to talk to. So, he asked if we would go and minister to her the next morning.

We arrived there and found out that she was not working, but was home sick. We knew then that God must have another purpose for us being there. As we were having our breakfast a group of business people came in and sat down at the table beside us. My attention was drawn to a certain man sitting at the end of the table. Shortly after that the Lord told me that He wanted me to give him a message from Him. After eating breakfast our friend needed to leave, so we walked him out to the lobby. I mentioned that I needed to hang around to get this message to this businessman.

The message was: "If you look to Me for the answer you need to make, then I will give you the wisdom you need to make the right decision." I wrote the message down on paper because they seemed to be in deep discussion. I marched the note down to the table, tapped the man on the shoulder and said, "excuse me, I'm a minister and I was sitting beside you and the Lord told me to give you a word from Him today." He looked at me with a smile and said, "thank you," while the others just stared at me.

We left the restaurant and as we were driving away, the man came out the restaurant. We knew he wanted us to stop, so we pulled over and he said, "thank you, this is the best news I've heard in a year. I have been working hard all year to get to where I am today and I'm getting ready to go to Bible school. I really needed to hear this!" The Lord spoke one more word to him as I pointed to the restaurant where his business partners were; "Don't look to the heart of man for answers, but get the heart of God—the answer that He will give you will bring you to the top."

Praise God! He was very excited and knew that God had visited him. We know that this will be a great testimony to those business associates of his that may not be Christians. God pointed him out in the restaurant in front of his colleagues. And one day, we believe, they will see that the hand of God has put him on top.

You're under arrest – literally

The Lord took me to downtown St. Paul and led me to a gentleman that was standing on a corner. He may have been selling drugs; I didn't think about it at the time, but looking back, he probably was. I went up to him and began to talk to him. It seemed as though he had built a huge wall between us, but I wasn't going to let it stop me. I kept giving him the Word of God, which is like a hammer to break down the wall. He told me to leave but the Holy Ghost wouldn't let me leave. No matter what, when the Lord says, "stay," you need to stay.

I wouldn't leave, so he left. I followed him to the other side of the street. I continued to talk to him, not to pester him, but because God was leading me to. I told him how urgent it was for him to give his life over to Jesus.

All of a sudden two guys quickly came out of the building that we were standing by. They looked kind of nervous as they looked at me and said, "Who are you?"

I said, "Ah, just preaching the Gospel." As I said that, I watched them put handcuffs on the gentleman I had been ministering to and take him away. They were two undercover policemen who arrested him right there as I was preaching to him. God got the Gospel into that man before he was arrested. The Lord knew what was about to happen. Even though he kept on saying, "Get away," there are some times you need to press in.

There he is...again

I met an old High School acquaintance in a restaurant, but wasn't able to talk with him very long—only a few minutes.

A few months later, I saw him on the road driving past me. I said, "God, here he is again: obviously it's not a coincidence, but I can't talk to him!" He said, "Pray for him."

Later on that summer we went to the State Fair to minister to people and I saw him there with a friend.

He asked, "What are you doing?"

So, I told him, "I'm sharing the Good News with people."

"Oh," he responded.

I talked to them about the relationship they needed to have with the Lord. They were attentive to what I said; it was obvious the Holy Spirit had gotten a hold of them. They received the Lord that night and I got to see the fruit of my prayers! Praise the Lord!

A shoulder to cry on

On my way home one night, my route led me right around downtown. I was on the freeway and I thought to myself, "Well, I'm just gonna go straight home." And God spoke to me and said, "No, you're not; you're going downtown." I thought, "Hmm."

I got off the exit ramp into downtown and knew that God had someone for me to minister to. I drove where I sensed the leading of the Lord bringing me and He brought me over by the Greyhound bus depot.

I hadn't parked yet, but the Lord drew my attention to a lady walking down the road. By the time I was able to park, I didn't know where that lady had gone to. I went over to the bus depot and began to minister to someone else. As I did, that lady came walking up. She looked very distressed; she had been drinking some and had been crying.

She asked a man beside me for a quarter for the telephone. He actually laughed at her; I guess he just thought she looked distressed because she had been drinking. But it happened that her brother had passed away the night before and she had come from Chicago to be with her family.

She needed to call her mother to get a ride. God had brought me down there just at that right time to meet her.

I decided to bring her to her mother's house. I had an opportunity to minister and pray for her. She prayed and received Jesus as her Lord and Savior for the first time that night. I prayed for the hurts that were in her heart and for the distress that she was going through. We always have to be ready to minister to someone in need.

No fear, Doctor Jesus is here!

The Holy Spirit said, "I want you to go to St. Paul." After pulling out a map, God showed me the exact location where He wanted us to go. We went down there, pulled up to some apartments and went around the back. I saw this man walking towards us as we were driving—there was something about him that I was drawn to. "I'm going to park the car; why don't you go and start talking to him," I said.

"This is Jeff; he's a born-again Christian. He is going into surgery tomorrow and he's got some fear about it." Then we found out that he put off the surgery on his spine for years because of that fear. After encouraging him, we prayed and laid our hands on him for healing. We felt the power of God. We believed that when he went in, the doctors were going to send him home because he was healed. We were rejoicing with him! He was free from fear, and it was awesome!

Jeff kind of laughed and said, "You know what? I'm going to track you down to let you know that God healed me."

Here's some coffee, let's talk

I heard in my spirit, "I'm sending you down to Maryland Avenue." On the way down, the Holy Ghost took control of us as we drove the car. At one intersection, our heads turned real quick to the left and we went, "Woo!" at the same time. Needless to say, we knew we needed to go left at that intersection. Then the Holy Spirit led us to a house and told us to let the people know that He sent us to them.

A gentleman came to the door; I gave him a tract and said, "the Holy Ghost sent us." The man paused for one second and said, "Do you want some coffee?" So all four of us went into the house and he proceeded to make us coffee and tea.

One of the team members led this man to Jesus for the very first time. He had such a sincere heart. Then we ministered to his backslidden daughter who was pregnant and had been recently involved in the occult. She made a renewed commitment to the Lord. What a great way to spend the night; watching a father and his daughter come to Jesus!

...If you have never made Jesus the Lord of your life, now is the time. He is waiting for you to totally commit your life to Him. He died on a cross to pay the price for sin and every wrong thing you have done. Three days later God raised Him from the dead and now He desires to live in your heart. Now, from your heart pray, "Jesus be my Lord. Forgive me of everything that I have done that You did not want me to do. Help me to live for You everyday; I love You."

(See II Corinthians 5:17-21, Romans 6:23 and 10:9-10)

Conclusion

The Holy Spirit is calling us to reach out to and encourage the broken hearted, the sick in body, the tormented, those in bondage, the rejected, the poor in spirit, the depressed, the homeless, the needy, the lonely, the hurting, the prodigal son or daughter, the ugly, the beautiful, the rich, the poor, the big, the small, the drunk, the abandoned, the disappointed, the crippled, the old, the young, the addict, the criminal, the body of Christ, and people of all the world. Are they not worth it? My God has created each one, knows of each one, loves each one, and is awaiting each one—that they may know Him and be free indeed!

... Go, therefore and make disciples of all nations, baptizing them in the name of the Father, and the Son and the Holy Spirit, teaching them to observe all things that I have commanded you; and lo, I am with you always, even to the end of the age." Amen. (Matthew 28:19-20)

-Jesus

New Wine Ministries
International

**PO Box 240932
Apple Valley, MN 55124**

www.newwineintl.org

If you would like to have Josh & Maureen speak at your church or gathering, please contact them at the above address or webpage.